To Nourish Any Flower
The Request Collection

by Tom Hegg
illustrated by Warren Hanson

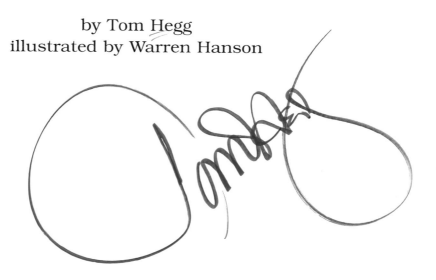

Waldman House Press, Inc.
Minneapolis

This book is dedicated
to the author's mother, Jeanette,
and to the illustrator's mother, Grace ...
the fairest flowers of them all.

Waldman House Press, Inc.
525 North Third Street
Minneapolis, Minnesota 55401

*T*his collection of poems
has been arranged in affectionate
response to the requests of many
people who have attended my
concerts over the years.
What a pleasure it has been
to share my work with live
audiences, and what an honor
to have received such
encouragement from them.
May these pieces give to
the reader at least a portion of
the joy that I have known in
creating and performing them.

–T.H.

To Nourish
Any Flower

This poem, inspired by my students, came to me in bits and pieces over the space of a decade. During that time, I went from apprentice to journeyman to master in the teaching profession. My title means, I believe, that I now have an appreciation for the vastness of what I have yet to learn.

"To Nourish Any Flower" touches on some of the timeless truths that a teacher can be lucky enough to catch — even on "those days" — in the faces of children.

To Nourish Any Flower

God has given all of us
    a measure of the Truth ...
An appetite for pleasure
    and the treasure of our youth ...

And nurture blends with nature
    through our days of taking root,
And attitudes commensurate
    most always follow suit.

To grow where you are planted
    can be something of a shock,
For some get sweetest loam,
    but some — a fissure in a rock.

Still, God has given all of us
    a measure of the Truth,
An appetite for pleasure
    and the treasure of our youth ...

And if you are exotic,
    in an out-or-inward way,
It may be one quixotic move
    to blossom and display.

The gentle scent that issues
    from the blooms along the rows ...
Those ruby-tinted tissues
    of the roses in repose

Become the favored diet
    of the masters of the land
Who might decide to quiet
    other blossoms with a hand

That rips away at slender veins ...
    that stems the surge and birth
Of innocents emerging
    from the tender bed of earth.

But God has given all of us
    a measure of the Truth,
An appetite for pleasure
    and the treasure of our youth.

Perhaps a different pungency
    should float upon the air ...
Reminding all who breathe it in
    that other kinds are there ...

And multicolored petals
    needn't frighten one at all ...
Nor those that bloom at night,
    nor those that flourish in the fall.

To nourish any flower
    is to thank our common source,
While honoring the sanctity of life
    that runs its course.

For God has given all of us
    a measure of the Truth,
An appetite for pleasure,
    and the treasure of our youth.

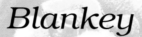

Blankey

Aside from "A Cup of Christmas Tea,"
"Blankey" is the oldest poem in my
repertoire and probably the one most
frequently requested. Although much of
its meaning is quite clear on the first
reading, it has resonances that I am still
discovering today. Sometimes it isn't
easy being a grown-up.

Blankey

I remember years ago when I was tiny ...
When my teeth and hair and outlook
    still were shiny ...
Whenever I got scared or hurt or cranky,
Next to Mom, my very best friend was
    ... my Blankey.

He was blue and worn and torn
    and frayed and tattered ...
Only grown-ups thought that those things
    ever mattered ...
But the night would lose its fright
    and softly hum
When I held my Blankey tight
    and "thucked my thumb."

Bit by bit I grew and bloomed
    and groomed my diction
As my Blankey felt the ravages of friction ...
And, as all good Blankeys must,
    he turned to rags and then, to dust ...

And without my friend to hold,
    life became a bit more cold.

It dawned on me, as I was eating candy ...
(After dinner, coffee, cigarettes and brandy),
That the things I sometimes use,
    (like the java, smoke and booze),
Plus some others I could list, just exist
    'cause Blankey's missed ...

I wonder ... could I make the old connection
If, in some fantastic woolly resurrection,
Blankey came back — warp and woof —
    and of course to make the proof,
We would lie quite still ... but then,
    would that magic work again?

I'll never know the answer to that question.
Boy, I'll tell you now, I'm open to suggestion.
You've got to think I'm bordering psychotic
Going on and on about a cloth narcotic.

They say what Blankey freed
    is still inside me …
And I must search for it
    without a thumb to guide me.
I'll find that "something" I have missed
Without my flannel catalyst
If I can find the guts to dare …
Well, maybe that's the answer, there.

I'm Going Bald

Even after I had written this poem, which is something of a minor prayer for the acceptance of my lot in life, I was still attempting to "cure" my ever-advancing baldness. So far, I have pursued vanity in vain. All my attempts at wiggery have been laughable. All the goop, glop and gunk on which I have spent good money have been no more effective than medicine-show snake oils. Maybe I should read this poem one more time …

I'm Going Bald

I'm going bald. I'm going bald.
Well, so what else is new?
I've been going bald
    since I was barely twenty-two.

Some days it deeply bothers me.
Some days I just don't care.
Some days I wonder when my scalp
    will be completely bare.

My mother has ten pounds of hair.
My father still has lots.
Some whimsical recessive gene
    is calling all my shots.

So why not use minoxidil,
    or some such other balm?
With my luck I would rub it in
    then grow hair on my palm.

God bless my balding brethren.
May we all find peace of mind.
May we bear with grace the jibes like,
    "Hey! You got shined!"

Let me not to self-delusion
    be completely led …
For if I must give up my hair,
    I fain would keep my head.

Deliver me from vanity,
    O Author of my fate,
And help me walk with sanity
    beneath my balding pate.

Teddy Bear

"Teddy Bear" is from a cycle of concert poems called "Moving Days." Together, they tell the story of a couple who faces the necessity of leaving a home that they have occupied for fifty years.

There are strongly autobiographical elements here. The actual move from my parents' house was a kind of Hegg family archaeological dig. Try as we did, we couldn't quite bring ourselves to throw away everything that we had accumulated. This passage focuses on one small item that had a stronger claim on me than I had thought.

Teddy Bear

I saw him on a basement shelf
    between some toys and books ...
I winced a little at the way
    the years had changed his looks ...

Neglect had dimmed the lustre
    of his brown and plushy pile ...
A frown was on the face
    that always mustered up a smile.

I lifted him and felt his head roll
    slowly to one side ...
His black eyes, scratched to cataracts,
    now lacked that spark of pride.

The dank and musty air
    had permeated every thread ...
How differently he'd smelled
    when he adorned my childhood bed.

How could I have let him come
    to such a shabby end?
My soul-mate ... my companion
    and my ever-loyal friend.

He was the commander
    of my legion of stuffed toys ...
An army quite the envy
    of the neighbor girls and boys ...

With one of Mom's discarded scarves
    tied tightly 'round his neck,
He could fly — as Super Bear —
    and keep the creeps in check.

On Christmases and birthdays
    brighter things would take his place ...
He bore it all with dignity,
    long-suffering and grace ...

And when the shallow substance
    of the new things came to light,
Old Teddy would resume his post
    beside me in the night.

He never really blamed me
    for the lousy things I did ...
He realized that I was only human,
    and a kid ...

We talked about my fickleness ...
    about respect and truth ...
We hugged and chalked it up
    to inexperience and youth.

I held him up ... this tattered totem
    of my growing stage ...
His plushy cloth integrity
    quite compromised by age ...

A dreadful rent had hemorrhaged
    some stuffing in his back ...
There wasn't time enough
    to spend repairing time's attack ...

The best thing I could do was toss him
    just one final time
Right in the plastic garbage bag
    with all the trash and grime.

I clenched my teeth and did it ...
    felt a deep stab of remorse ...
I told myself,
    "This isn't an interment or divorce!

Save your tortured feelings
    for events that matter more,
And not for throwing ancient junk
    outside the back screen door."

I did my best to flog it all away —
    out of my mind —
I made this silent pledge:
    "Whatever else that I might find,

It goes into the dumpster.
    I'll be ruthless! I'll be hard!"
At nine that night I had it all
    bagged up in the back yard.

I went to bed ... I tossed and turned ...
    I got back up, and then ...
I went outside
    to search for my lost Teddy Bear again.

The Big Front Door

"The Big Front Door" is the final portion of "Moving Days." I still have occasion to drive past what was, for so many years, our family's home. Time has taken the sting away, and the muscle memory that once told me to pull into that driveway is long gone. I still remember, though … and I'm glad I do.

The Big Front Door

Everything was out at last.
    The folks were on their way.
I was plain exhausted.
    It had been a draining day.

The endless crates ...
    the sheer, back-busting labor of it all ...
The fussing and adjusting ...
    I had scarcely strength to crawl.

A single job remained ...
    to close and lock the big front door.
That may sound simple but it is, in fact,
    a taxing chore ...

You have to first finesse the key
    into the tricky lock
And press against the door
    to let the bolt slide past a block ...

The door was in good form just then ...
    it put up quite a fight ...
The lock refused to turn —
    "Pure stubbornness!" I thought,
    "Pure spite!"

And as I wrestled with the door
    (which had me well outclassed),
I realized that this would be our final fight …
    our last.

I paused and thought,
    "How many times
    has this same scene been played?"
That door withstood, with will and wood,
    the years — and threats — we made.

We vowed a thousand times
    that we'd replace it with a door
That knew its place and locked with grace
    and wouldn't ask for more.

We never did it. Why? Don't ask …
    I haven't got a clue …
I guess it was a thing
    we somehow couldn't seem to do.

I caught my breath and said,
    "Let's give the darn thing one more try."
I pushed again —
    and then I thought,
    "I haven't said goodbye."

"That's crazy!" said the Voice of Reason,
    rushing to the fore,
"I simply can't allow you
    to get soft about a door!

To be a little misty over moving day is fine,
But getting soppy over doors
    is where I draw the line!"

Perhaps I came unbalanced for a moment.
    That could be.
I saw the valanced entryway ...
    and saw it look at me.

It's seen me come and go.
    It's guarded everyone I've loved.
It opens on its own strict terms ...
    when prodded, pushed and shoved.

I've swung upon its hinges
    as a playful little boy ...
It's let me in in deep despair
    and let me in in joy ...

It knows me as a prodigal ...
    it knows me as a dad ...
I know it as my Big Front Door ...
    the first I ever had.

I stood there like a perfect fool.
    I tried so not to cry …
I touched the weathered wood
    and then I said, at last,
    "Goodbye."

I pulled it shut.
    With utter ease,
    the key turned in the lock!
It clicked with sweet efficiency!
    I stood in total shock …

I turned away …
    and saw a vision coming up the walk …
The buyer and his family!
    I hoped that I could talk.

Their faces were bright with eagerness,
    in sharp contrast to mine …
They asked if I was feeling well.
    I said, "Oh, yes … I'm fine …

It's only that this move
    has knocked the stuffing out of me."
They kindly said they understood.
    I handed them the key.

I wished them well. They did the same.
   I got into my car ...
I waved and rolled away ... and then,
   before I got too far,

I looked again ... and saw
   what I'd been somehow hoping for ...
There in my rear-view mirror ...
   They were struggling with the door.

To Teachers

As my teaching career continues, I have a greater and greater respect for the people who were once my own teachers. Time has carried many of them away.

I'll never forget the moment when I learned that my high school choir teacher, Oscar B. Dahle, had died. Twenty years had passed since my graduation, but that didn't matter. O.B.D. had become a permanent, inevitable fixture in my mind and in the minds of thousands and thousands of people whose lives had been touched by his. I remember thinking, "This can't be! Who's going to be in charge now?"

We, his students, alternately worshiped and were exasperated by this demanding, loving man (who could be pretty scary when he wanted to be!) His death was obviously a mistake. I could no more conceive of a world without him than I could imagine it without sky or the color green. He cared deeply, profoundly and particularly about developing the compassion and dignity of each of the children in his classroom. No teacher I have ever met — before or since — has been so brilliantly able to save kids by getting across the joy of taking something beyond themselves seriously.

How many of us — foolishly bent on having mere "fun" — owe our very humanity to this man … and to other teachers like him? I dare to hope that when I am at my best, there are echoes of his voice in mine.

To Teachers

You taught me how to take a stand.
    You taught me right from wrong.
You firmly took me by the hand
    and made me learn that song.

You taught me art and history
    and metal shop and wood …
And when I only got a "C",
    you still said I was good.

You taught me how to cook and sew …
    you taught me how to drive …
You took the time to let me know
    you cared I was alive …

You yelled at me and made me see
    that I was not alone …
And I should never merely be
    the sum of all I own.

You made me mad with all your rules:
    "Use pencil, and not ink!"
You said a million times that school's
    "A place where one must think!"

So now, I think I'll thank you
    for the privilege to choose …
For all the work you put me through
    I thought I'd never use …

And all I thought irrelevant …
    and all I thought a sham …
In spite of my resistance
    went to make me who I am:

A person of civility …
    of conscience truly tried …
A person of humility …
    of confidence and pride.

You taught me how to take a stand.
    You taught me right from wrong.
You firmly took me by the hand …
    and made me learn that song.

Refrigerator Art

The primary purpose of a refrigerator (as anyone who knows a child well enough will agree) is not to keep food cold. It is, rather, to display the artwork of a child. A good curator will have a variety of magnets on hand at all times.

Refrigerator Art

Red and yellow, green and blue ...
Streaks and smears and globs of glue ...
"Lookit, Daddy! It's for you!"
Refrigerator Art.

Cotton clouds on tempera skies ...
Clowns with M&Ms for eyes ...
"Don't tell Mommy! It's a s'prise!"
Refrigerator Art.

Sometimes it takes a bit of care
To see the horsey he sees there ...
He sure sees more than WE see where
Imagination counts.

Giggles in the squiggled lines ...
Multicolored glitter shines
On birthday cards and valentines
In copious amounts.

No perspective. No technique.
Far from perfect. Far from chic.
Love alone makes them unique ...
Refrigerator Art.

A Mother Waits

In honor of our mothers, to whom this book is dedicated, Warren and I wanted to include a piece having directly to do with motherhood. As I cast my mind's eye over the span of a parent's life, I observe that much of our time is spent in the process of waiting. Sometimes a wait is pleasant … even delicious. Sometimes a wait is a painful trial. The waits I have seen mothers go through seem to be the most vivid of all. Mom, I hope you hear the love in this poem. Sorry to have kept you waiting.

A Mother Waits

A mother waits to hear if everything
    will be alright.
She waits throughout the day
    and then she waits throughout the night.

A mother waits beside the phone.
    She waits beside the bed.
She waits and wonders if you meant
    the wild words you said.

She waits until the children say,
    "Okay! Now you can look!"
She waits until her work is done
    before she reads her book.

She waits for news. She waits for signs.
    She waits inside the car.
She waits because you're late
    and wonders where on earth you are.

She waits until the test results are in.
    She stands and waits
Beside a window as the light reflects
    off empty plates.

She waits in line. She waits her turn.
    She waits behind the door.
She talks you into waiting just
    a couple hours more.

She waits until she hears the sound
    of one familiar voice.
She waits because she wants to
    and because she has no choice.

A mother waits for miracles.
    A mother waits until
The waiting's over.
    Then, for all we know, she's waiting still.

God has given all of us
        a measure of the Truth ...
An appetite for pleasure
        and the treasure of our youth ...

Tom Hegg, author of the much-loved A CUP OF CHRISTMAS TEA, is a writer, teacher, actor, husband and father. Trained for the classical repertory stage at Carnegie-Mellon University and the University of Minnesota, he spent five seasons with the Tyrone Guthrie Theatre in Minneapolis.

Tom teaches drama at Breck School these days, and has recently been awarded the title of Master Teacher. He has also been named a Teacher of Excellence and an Honor Roll Teacher by the Minnesota Education Association. He is a prominent public speaker and is also heard on national and international radio and television shows.

TO NOURISH ANY FLOWER is his fourth collaboration with Warren Hanson, following THE MARK OF THE MAKER and UP TO THE LAKE. The Heggs — Tom, Peggy and Adam — make their home in Eden Prairie, Minnesota.

Warren Hanson has spent the last twenty years in his home studio, doing what he has loved since childhood — drawing. In addition to illustrating the words of Tom Hegg, Warren is a writer himself. He writes a humor column for his neighborhood newspaper, and has recently written and illustrated A IS FOR ADULT, an alphabet book for grown-ups.

Warren graduated with a theater degree from Augustana College, and received his art education at the College of Associated Arts in St. Paul, Minnesota, where he has also taught and is currently chairman of the board of trustees. Warren lives in St. Paul with his wife, Patty, and his two children, Cody and Lacey.

ACKNOWLEDGEMENTS

The author and illustrator would like to express great and abiding thanks to Ned and Brett Waldman, the father and the son who know so well what it means To Nourish Any Flower. Shalom.